Let Love Grow

Elizah Peterson

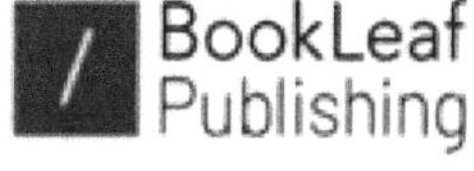

Presentation by *BookLeaf Publishing*

Web: www.bookleafpub.com

E-mail: info@bookleafpub.com

ISBN: 9789357211390

First edition 2022

DEDICATION

I would like to Dedicate this book to the Moon, to the Sun, to the stars that light up the midnight sky.

You have Always been there.

You are Constant.

You are Reliable.

You Provide.

Through it All...

You have been The Truth.

I would also Love to Dedicate this book to Kevin and Kelly Einsel.

Nino, Nina..

Thank you for your Time, Your Heart, Your Forgiveness, Your Advice and Your Love for My Family.

Thank You, For Always being there for me

Always listening, and Thank you for letting me grow up with you.

ACKNOWLEDGEMENT

I would like to acknowledge my struggles.
My hard times. My poor decisions and choices.
I would like to acknowledge my immaturity and
lack of understanding.
Ignoring the sound advice given time and time
again.

I would like to acknowledge my bravery. Taking
risks.
My travels, encounters, experiences.
I would like to acknowledge my thirst for
Learning,
My hunger for Universal Truth,
I would like to acknowledge my perseverance.

Without these choices, without these
experiences, I would not be who I am today.
I am proud of who I am Today.

PREFACE

May others feel Relatability,
May others see The Struggle.
May others find Understandability,
A Lovely Life amidst the Rubble.

The Paper

I escape from real life,
By my words and feelings
I get lost in another land,
With my mind and a pen

The Paper seems too bare,
So I fill it with my thoughts and dreams

It calls out to me to fill it's pages
The paper knows me better than I know myself
It knows my deepest secrets
My most inner thoughts
My mind boggling thoughts
The things I hope and long for

It knows the very things that haunt my soul
My fears, joys and actions.
The paper knows me inside and out
Better than anyone can ever know me

Value Of Voice

Value of music
Value of voice
How important are these
In the audio world?
If you have the words,
Why need the music?
Are audible words required,
To hold a conversation?

A look in one's eyes
Down into their soul
Can speak volumes
The simple Act of love
Speaks louder

An Act of forgiveness
Mercy, joy and patience
A sweet smile speaks forever
A hug goes on for eternity
The breaking of bread
A moment of silence
A wave "Hello"
A friendly nod in one's direction

To acknowledge a Life..

A Value

Pandemic Poetry 2

There is a Divide.
A sickness of the mind
The pressure to choose and,
The consequences
Are life and death

My body
My choice
Your body
My choice

Choose right
or Die
Choose My Way
Or walk away

Obey or Leave
Unfriend
Disassociate
Starve
Die
Or Fight

Poetry

Relatability.

Comfortability and,

The Ability

To Take an experience,
The thoughts, feelings, emotions and,
Transmit them into words

Time

Time is a beautiful thing

Sometimes it is hard to think
Of time as a Thing, sure.
We are all living and experiencing life..

Time just Happens.

So many amazing things can happen
In Time.

Growth Always happens,
Positive or Negative.

Sometimes all Something needs is,
Time.

This or That

Where do I fit in, in this world?
If you're not divided by religion
You're divided by color

Red, Yellow, Purple
I was too black for the whites
Too white for the blacks
Too brown for them both

There was a war in me
Two worlds clashing together
Yet neither captivating my heart.

My Red, Red Heart.

I was a host
A mirage in the distance
You saw me but, what you saw,
Was not really there

I was not This
I was not That
I am not "Brown"
I am not "Black"

Re-Routed

My world was so vivid
So full of color
Bright colors, deep colors,
Not one was like the other

Clouds were puffy and white
Rain was cold and wet
Sunny days were Oh so hot
The sun would rise and set

The moon would shine in the sky
The stars would twinkle about,
The crickets would whisper at night
The morning brought the rooster to shout

I heard things
I saw things
I believed In so much

That may have not really been there

Questions

There's an urgency
To beat the clock
The clock of time
Of space
To figure it all out
"Figure out what?" you say..

I don't know.
I'm trying to figure it out.

Where did the sun come from?
Who lit up the moon?
What Really is,
The Solar System?
Who is Out There?
There Has to be More.

But there's a Timer.
And I've wasted so much.

Every day I feel closer
Every day there are clues
Yet, there is still so much
I just do not know.

Time will run out,
My questions, just notes
The answers will have escaped me and,
My curiosities up in smoke

Aries

A raging fire am I
Burning hot, burning bright
Consuming everything in my path
My pace is fast
My flames take flight
Swallowing thoughts
Feelings, emotions
Ideas, wants, needs
Growing stronger
Growing hotter
Always wanting more

A yearning deep within

To sit
To be calmed
To submit
To serve
To give

To Love

I see

I have walked a different journey
More different than the norm
I have met many people, seen many places
Yet never stopped long to conform

One day I passed a tree
Which looked very different from the rest
The fruit it gave
The leaves it shed
The giving of it's best

This tree has a different purpose
 A complex design and creed
This tree desires to grow a forest
And knows it starts with a seed

I have to acknowledge the past,
The origins of this particular tree
The planting, the watering and patience
To see the beauty I now see

Colorful World

Such a detailed, full world.
A clear, concise past, present and future
I felt I knew who I was
Where I came from and,
Where I was going

Then, things began to disappear.
Little by little, one by one
Colors faded to nothing,
Timelines began to shift
People, history and events
Faded to invisibility

Grasping, reaching for footing,
But it all disappeared.
Everything I stood so firmly for,
Everything I loved and looked forward to,

Gone.

So here I stand,
Not a thing in sight.
No color, no form, no history or future
Hungry to know Truth
Longing for honest information

Desiring those colors once more
Waiting for answers
In this empty room

I Know

I know I love you
I know I do,
I want to be near you
To be held by you
But I know I need time
And to give Time a chance
I don't want to hurt you
Let's do a forever dance

I'll give the rainbow
The chance to shine
I'll let the earthworm
Find it's kind
I'll let the cornstalk grow
The rose time to bloom
The penguin the chance
To find it's home

And one day
I hope,
After the spider
Has spun it's web,
When the cows have come home
And the strawberries are red,

That you'll consider me as,
One that wants you,

And wants to see
The Beauty in you

Existence

There stands a Giant

A tree that towers homes,
Buildings and people

The people take cover
In the shade of it's leaves,
Basking in it's coolness
While the tree itself
Is burned from the sun
It's leaves heated
It's bark now dry

When the heat dissipates
And coolness comes about
The people cut the tree
They chop it's limbs
They tear it's leaves
They burn the off-shoots
To keep warm in the cold

This Giant never moves

It was planted for
The People

To Give
To Serve
Never to Take.

They may cut the Giant
To the floor one day,
This tree may no longer exist

Yet,
It Gave
Warmth
Shelter
Time

...It's Existence

Rest

Could you close your eyes
Just for a moment?
Could you rest those weary shoulders?
Can you ease your mind
Just this moment in time?
And leave this world behind?

Don't think about tomorrow
Don't think about the past
Don't think about the worries of today
Or your memories, happy or sad

Don't think about the world
And the insurmountable troubles it holds
The injustices, the pain
Don't let it all unfold

Know that I am here,
Rest in my Love for you
I want to see your dreams come true
And mine will come true too

Crumbs

The crumbs you threw my way
I know now they were bait
To soften my heart toward you
To seal your wounded fate

You say there are snakes in the Garden
A snake can recognize a snake

And you bit me.

So dazed and confused
Poison coursing my veins
And now I bleed out

You watch
You slide past me
Not a flinch in your body
Not a care in the world

I've learned
The Garden is not where I want to be
So, I'll leave.
I'll find my way out
Hopefully never to return

Lab Rat

I finally figured it out
And it no longer hurts my heart
I should have noticed all of the signs
That were right there from the start

A scientist observes
Their observations are from afar
Their interactions with the subject are few
As distant as the stars

Emotions and feelings are obsolete
When gathering information and data
Facts, stats and observations
Are a requirement for the matter

I've Won

There's always a castle
Far, far away
A witch with a spell
And a prince to save the day

A life of fairytales
We are promised
One of magic, miracles and love
One which ensures that
Dreams come true, that there's
A man in the moon
That the dish ran away with the spoon

But what if
The prince doesn't come
The dream falls apart
The world weighs a ton
No one tells you that part

Well, This Princess Works
She gets her silver and gold
At the crack of dawn
You know she's gone
This homeschool mom
She's on the run

To make it fun
For her young ones
My Daughter, My Son,
I feel I've Won

You are my Castle
You are my Magic
You are my Potion in a bottle.
You are my Wish upon a star
You are my Happily Ever After

Cheyanne

Dear Mom and Dad,
I just wanted to say,
Thank you for adopting my sister.
I know I begged you
Over and over
For a sister
She's pretty great.
She's pretty strong.
I'm Really proud of her.
Mom, now that you're gone,
Life can get really lonely.
I'm so grateful
I have her
She shares my pain,
She shares my sorrow.
She's a mom now too.
I have a niece!
I have a nephew!
I love them so much.
I feel like she's my Gift.
She's Beautiful
Like an angel
She's Fierce
I love My Sister

Trust Again

How do you heal
A Fallen tree?

How do you mend
It's broken roots?

How do you remind it
Of it's stature,
It's power and beauty?

A breathing branch
Is painfully picked
Planted in a new grove
And is left to live again,
To trust again
Trust growth
Trust the sun
To trust in Time.
All the while knowing
The grand tower it can be,
Knowing where it came from
And who it can Be

Abide In You

We're Here
Watching over you
Guiding you
Showing you
Waking you
To the Truth

The Truth of,
Our Reality
The reality of Those
Before Us
The reality that is,
And will be Yours

Slow down, Sweet soul
Gather around the fire
Take notice of the sun's arrival and,
The sun's descent

Consume the moonlight
The stars and dark skies
Be One with the Earth
The soil beneath your feet

You descend from Our Blood

You have Our Eyes
You see what we saw
Your body tells Our Story
Your existence proves..
Our existence
Our fight

We never left
We are Here
In You

So,
Fight.
Stand up
Be a Voice

The Warrior in Us
The Warriors Before Us
Abide in You

Planted

A newborn baby has no idea
That one day they will walk
They do not comprehend
Their cries will evolve to talk

The seed of a crispy, sweet apple
Planted gently in the earth
Feels darkness, water and dirt
Unaware of the greatness it shall birth

A brightly colored set of yarn,
Cannot imagine it's beauty
Of what it possibly can become.
Yet when it has fulfilled an imagination,
It is a masterpiece of art,
With many plans and uses

It takes outside forces
To help grow or create Anything
To come to fruition

A garden may look beautiful,
Producing many healthy soils and flowers,
The garden took time and transformation
The garden ingested water and sunshine

It endured pruning and transplanting
Resulting in variety, color and beauty

A Woman,
Has the ability to become So Much.
There are so many hidden paths within her.
Outside forces can determine life and death for
her.
She can fulfill so many roles.
A daughter, a sister, a friend, a mother.
Things and people can be taken from her.
She does not know what she is capable of,
Until it is her day to endure it.
She can be stripped of all she knows,
Taking the paths of new beginnings
Not knowing the strength inside herself
Unaware of what or who she is capable of
becoming.

Yet, it Happens...
Through the darkness, water and dirt..
With the help of a little sunshine and blue skies,

She emerges.